Standing
In
The Gap

Standing
In
The Gap

By

Don Gilmore

CHRISTIAN • LITERATURE • CRUSADE
Fort Washington, Pennsylvania 19034

CHRISTIAN LITERATURE CRUSADE

U.S.A.
Box 1449, Ft. Washington, PA 19034

© 1991 Don Gilmore

ISBN 0-87508-178-9

Scripture quotations in this publication, *unless otherwise marked*, are from the *Holy Bible, New International Version*. Copyright © 1973, 1978, International Bible Society.

Other quotations from:
The King James Version of the Bible (*KJ*).
The New King James Version (*NKJ*). Copyright © 1979, 1980, 1982, Thomas Nelson, Inc., Publishers.
The Amplified Bible (*Amp*). *The Amplified Old Testament*, copyright © 1965, 1987 by the Zondervan Corporation. *The Amplified New Testament*, copyright © 1958, 1987 by the Lockman Foundation. Used by permission.
The Living Bible (*LB*). Copyright © 1971, Tyndale House Publishers, Wheaton, IL 60187.
The Holy Bible, Revised Standard Version (*RS*). Old Testament Section, copyright 1952 and New Testament Section, copyright 1946, by Division of Christian Education of the National Council of the Churches of Christ in the U.S.A. Thomas Nelson & Sons, New York.

Cover photo: Superstock/Dennis Junor

Printed in the United States of America

CONTENTS

INTRODUCTION

The 22nd chapter of the Book of Ezekiel contains some of the strongest language in the Bible. The judgment of God is heard thundering against His people, accusing them of a whole catalogue of sins. Then come the deeply moving words of verse 30, poignantly revealing the very heart of God:

And I sought for a man among them, that should make up the hedge, and stand in the gap before me for the land, that I should not destroy it: but I found none.[1]

With great anguish the Lord God had watched His beloved human family sinfully misusing their free will—breaking down the spiritual "hedge"[2] that protected them from the wrath of His judgment. The Lord's saving solution was to call for someone obediently to "stand in the gap,"[3] as an "intercessor"[4] or interceder before Him on behalf of sinful humanity.

"The gap" as defined in the original language was a hole in the wall of an armed city resulting from incessant battering by a military assault weapon. In times of siege, many places along a city wall would come under attack until one gave way, allowing enemy troops to pour through the breach.

The prophet Ezekiel was aware that the forces

[1]Ezekiel 22:30, *KJ* [2]Job 1:10 [3]Ezekiel 22:30, *KJ* [4]Isaiah 59:16, *KJ*

of evil had broken down the spiritual, ideological defenses of his people. Corruption, injustice, immorality were smashing against the walls of the national government, religious institutions, family life, environment and the common life of his people. The enemy, having succeeded in breaching the wall, was now spilling through.

God called to "His own"[5] to "stand in the gap"; to become a human wall of resistant faith; to exercise reliance on the spiritual-moral weaponry of God; to offer sacrificial devotion in serving the public good; but no one volunteered—not one—until years later when Jesus came. He came not only to stand in the gap for people of His own day, but by His absolutely unique, loving, atoning, forgiving, ransoming death on the cross, He remains humanity's saving intercessor forever. Not only that, He left us His example.[6]

Now at this moment in the history of our planet the human family is again being challenged by an emergency appeal from Almighty God to follow the example of Jesus. We are exhorted ". . . first of all, that requests, prayers, intercession and thanksgiving be made for everyone. . . ."[7] This is a strategic work for those positioned in Christ, whose hearts have been broken by the sinful condition of this world—and who know beyond any shadow of doubt that standing in the intercessory prayer gap, come hell or high water, is exactly what God wants us to do.

Consider how we got into the shape we're in. In the beginning God gave His first Adam "dominion"[8] over the earth. Adam was in effect "lord" of this planet. Then came the event theologians

---

[5]John 1:11, *KJ*   [6]1 Peter 2:21, *KJ*   [7]1 Timothy 2:1
[8]Genesis 1:26–28, *KJ*

describe as "the fall of man."[9] In an exercise of earthshaking disobedience, Adam by default transferred his God-given superior authority in the order of creation to a lesser being, allowing Satan (the enemy of God) in the guise of a serpent to tell him (imagine—*him*) what to do!

Consequently, because of Adam's tragic abdication of authority and responsibility, Satan became "god of this world."[10] This is a fact that even Jesus Himself never disputed;[11] nor was it challenged in the post-crucifixion, resurrection, ascension era of the early church. Though Jesus did, in fact, decisively defeat Satan, "triumphing"[12] over him, nevertheless the adversary is still among us and, if anything, is gaining in strength and influence.

But how can a defeated enemy continue to expand his operation? The answer is simple. The "god of this world" has the staying power of a distant relative who comes to your house for a short weekend visit, then moves in, taking up residence indefinitely—eating your food, sleeping in your bed, driving your car, watching your TV, spending your money—*occupying your space*. When asked to leave, the request is ignored because he doesn't believe you're serious. The trouble is we've given him so much aid and comfort that we have in many instances become unintentional co-conspirators in his empire building.

Once again the Lord God is calling His people to "stand in the gap" on behalf of the rest of humanity. He's saying, "I need you; in fact, I've chosen to need you by limiting Myself to a part-

[9]Genesis 3:1–7 [10]2 Corinthians 4:4, *KJ* [11]Matthew 4:8–9 [12]Colossians 2:14–15

nership arrangement." Jesus compared this working relationship to that of a vine and its branches. He said, "I am the vine: you are the branches."[13] The vine supplies the branch with nourishing strength; but it's the branch that produces the fruit.

Our intercessory praying is the partnership production of fruit for carrying out God's will in the world. John Wesley, one of the saints of the church, once wrote, "It seems that God is limited by our prayer life. He can do nothing for humanity unless someone asks Him to do it." "Standing in the gap"—offering intercessory prayers for others—is asking Him to do it.

Intercessory prayer is the offering of our highest aspirations for someone or some situation as a "spiritual sacrifice." If our offering is accepted—if it fits the overall intent of God's will—it will be transformed by the touch of divine power and re-enter the stream of human experience as a flow of blessing—blessing which usually goes beyond the specifications of our intercession.

In order that you may pray more effectively as you stand in the intercessory gap, I'm going to propose a method of preparing yourself—a method that the Holy Spirit gave me during a critical intercessory challenge—which I have called "A Lesson in Prayer." After making your way through the several outlined steps, you will read a series of intercessory prayers in four major categories that, hopefully, will stimulate you to take your place in the ministry of intercessory prayer. As you read through the following prayers, notice the emphasis that I place on telling your own story to God in prayer, so that

[13]John 15:5

your prayer becomes an unvarnished expression of you as a person—as honest and straightforward as pouring out your heart to a trusted friend.

Anyone who's read King David's prayers in the Psalms has sampled the range, mood, and expression of a wonderfully open and confessing heart to God. David withheld nothing from the Lord, exposing every detail of his very human experience, writing it all down in the Psalm book which is the record of his devotional life. Presenting yourself to God in prayer, as it was with David, ought to be a totally honest confessional where imperfections, ambiguities, manipulations—even prayer manipulations—are set free to surface and be seen for what they are.

Prayer should also become a tool that on one end chisels away at hardened self-love deceptions and on the other end is a personally empowering connection with the Lord, enabling us to serve Him.

Let me add that over the past few years in preparation for praying I've devoted a chunk of priority time each day to reading from four sections of Scripture—two from the Old Testament: (1) Genesis through Esther and (2) Job through Malachi—and two from the New Testament: (1) The Gospels and (2) Acts through Revelation. I regularly listen to the Scriptures on cassette tape while reading—which adds an extra dimension to my devotions. While reading, I take notes in a prayer diary, citing verses which have special meaning, underscoring them and making comments. Then I talk to the Lord about the challenges of the day—problems I'm facing and needs to be met—all the time writing out each prayer. As I pray I attempt carefully to apply Scripture as often as I can to these needs. This is accomplished by working my way through the basic outline you will be reading shortly. Finally, I pray over an extensive intercessory prayer list containing names of people and concerns, applying Scripture, and closing off with songs of praise and thanksgiving.

Now, let me present the following outline for your practical use. Incidentally, all the following prayers employ the same general outline for their launching pad. While the following steps are not specifically spelled out in the prayers you'll be reading later on, they are certainly intrinsic parts of the whole.

FIRST: We need to address God as did the early Christian church: "O Sovereign Lord, You are He Who made the heaven and the earth and the sea and everything that is in them."[14] These thrilling words of worship provide an unlimited horizon for our praying. We are speaking to the CREATOR who is also OUR FATHER.

SECOND: We should always pray in the name of Jesus up front rather than relegating it to a sort of complimentary close. Praying in Jesus' name is to pray "in" all He is—all that He stands for. It's to recognize yourself as His representative here on earth. This is what it means to be "in Christ." Praying in His name is to pray according to His promise like this one: "And I will do whatever you ask in my name, so that the Son may bring glory to the Father. You may ask me for anything in my name, and I will do it."[15] Praying in His name is also praying in His nature—just as He would pray were He in your place right now. This one reminder goes a long way in iden-

[14]Acts 4:24, *Amp* [15]John 14:13–14

12

tifying and cleaning up much of the selfishness in our prayer life.

THIRD: As we draw near to God, we may be overwhelmed by the cold hard fact that we are sinners, separated from Him on any number of levels. Therefore we need to confess and receive cleansing. First John 1:9 helps magnificently. Positionally, this is where we should be in prayer—leaning on His mercy. Furthermore, while confessing, we need truly to forgive those with whom we've had personal problems. It's impossible to pray accurately and effectively while carrying hate or resentment in your heart.[16]

FOURTH: Please turn to Paul's letter to the Ephesians, chapter 6. It is absolutely essential that you put on the whole armor of God if you are going to get into serious prayer . . . which inevitably includes being involved in spiritual warfare. Carefully

> . . . [gird] your waist with truth, . . . put on the breastplate of righteousness, . . . [protect] your feet with the preparation of the gospel of peace, . . . take the shield of faith . . . and the helmet of salvation, and the sword of the Spirit, which is the word of God; praying always with all prayer and supplication in the Spirit, being watchful to this end with all perseverance and supplication for all the saints.[17]

FIFTH: It is necessary to take our God-given Christ-purchased authority as a believer and bind, rebuke, command, and cast out our adversary the Devil from the target area of our praying. It would be instructive to read Matthew 4

[16]Mark 11:25–26   [17]Ephesians 6:14–17, *NKJ*

several times. Note how Jesus dealt with Satan. Notice the way He used God's Word. Read in other places in the Gospel record how He cast out the enemy[18] and bound the negative influence. Please don't assume that just by quoting scripture at Satan, he'll automatically disappear. Be sure that your Scripture words are backed up by a life that is solidly anchored in the Lord.

SIXTH: Seek the guidance of the Holy Spirit[19] to help you choose the scriptures God would have you establish as a prayer platform—whatever the need. Your daily reading of the Bible ought to produce a variety of scriptures for that purpose. For instance, when I was praying for a woman in a stormy-night crisis situation a verse I'd worked through the day before grounded both of us: "I am the Lord, who heals you."[20] Standing on God's Word is an inspired strategy in waging warfare against that resistive force that contends against us.

SEVENTH: If possible, agree with someone in prayer. Remember Jesus' admonition:

> Again, I tell you that if two of you on earth agree about anything you ask for, it will be done for you by my Father in heaven. For where two or three come together in my name, there am I with them.[21]

Husbands and wives ought to agree in prayer on a regular basis as a means of multiplying their prayer power.[22] In fact, this is one of the main functions of a true marriage. If you're not married, find a prayer partner.

EIGHTH: Pray believingly! Jesus says:

[18]Like Matthew 12:29   [19]John 14:26   [20]Exodus 15:26
[21]Matthew 18:19–20   [22]1 Peter 3:7

Have faith in God, . . . I tell you the truth, if anyone says to this mountain, "Go, throw yourself into the sea," and does not doubt in his heart but believes that what he says will happen, it will be done for him. Therefore I tell you whatever you ask for in prayer, believe that you have received it, and it will be yours.[23]

Believing prayer is accompanied by faithful rejoicing that God has taken over the prayer need.

Rejoice in the Lord always. I will say it again: Rejoice! Let your gentleness be evident to all. The Lord is near. Do not be anxious about anything, but in everything, by prayer and petition, with thanksgiving, present your requests to God.[24]

Notice that part of rejoicing is giving thanks. We thank God that He has entered the praying process and is leading us to ultimate victory. It's not enough just to petition the Lord—it's equally important to adopt the attitude of faith assurance. If we are cleared for takeoff in prayer, we should let our prayer-engines be revved up to full expectancy. Then we move out trustingly toward our prayer objective.

NINTH: Be careful to seek God's will whatever your prayer project. There's nothing worse than praying for months and years about something that is out of His will. We need to stay in continual companionship with the Lord, reading His Word, walking in His way—so that we can pray as Godwardly as Jesus did in Gethsemane: "Father, if you are willing, take this cup from me; yet not my will, but yours be done."[25] In time,

[23]Mark 11:22–24 [24]Philippians 4:4–6 [25]Luke 22:42

we'll be praying more and more for those things we know are in accordance with His will. In that way, we are able to pray with increasing faith and trust.

TENTH: Let every prayer session end with praise.

> Through Jesus, therefore, let us continually offer to God a sacrifice of praise—the fruit of lips that confess His name.[26]

There is a wide variety of ways to praise the Lord. We can come before His presence with worship and praise through singing our faith.[27] We can come expressing our joy.[28] We can come bowing down.[29] We can come speaking praise.[30] We can come quietly and still.[31] Whatever the way—we come to worship our God.

I'm aware that these are not the only steps to a valid prayer life, but they are the ones I've tried and tested over the years and recommend to you from experience. Again, as you begin reading the upcoming intercessory prayers, please remember that the foregoing basic prayer outline has been employed in every instance.

Once more, let me challenge you, among other things, to write out your prayers. Tell your story to God and put your specific needs on paper. Rarely if ever do I write out the ten general steps; however, my prayer story and petitions are written and often rewritten so that they will represent the best intercessory sacrifice I can make to the Lord. Furthermore, the discipline of specifically writing your prayer is an effective means of defining more precisely what you are seeking, rather than rambling on and

[26]Hebrews 13:15 [27]Psalm 95:1 [28]Psalm 5:11 [29]Psalm 95:6
[30]Psalm 134:1 [31]Psalm 46:10

on. May I suggest that if you are praying for a specific person, you might give him a copy of your prayer to help him pray in agreement with you.

PRAYING FOR THE CHURCH

A CRITICAL SPIRIT

Lord, she's upset again! This time it's the pulpit deacon's poor tie selection. Last time it was his coat. Before that it was the song leader throwing his arms around, or the color of the flowers on the altar, or the temperature of the sanctuary, or the volume of the organ, or the choice of anthems, or a deacon's style of ushering, or babies crying during worship, or too many people in church—or too few!

I intercede for this self-appointed critic who constantly chooses to sit in "the seat of the scornful"[1] as the "body"[2] assembles for worship.

I speak to the controlling influence in that person's life, "I command you (critical spirit) in the name of Jesus Christ, come out of her."

Lord, I pray for Your healing resurrection spirit to flow through this woman who's been coming to worship on unbended knee, with a stiff neck.[3] I pray to see a change in her attitude and life by the power of Jesus' name.

[1]Psalm 1:1, *KJ* [2]1 Corinthians 12:27, *KJ* [3]Psalm 75:5, *KJ*

REALLY, LORD?!

Lord, I've been interceding for this woman with great anguish, trying to get her to You. So far I haven't even gotten her to church. What now, Lord?

I really do have faith that one day she'll make a total commitment to You.[1] Meanwhile, what should I do? What techniques should I apply?

No techniques? What, then?

You want me to treat her like she's already committed? You want me to ask her to pray for others, just like I'd do with any other Christian, and to occasionally grab her hand and pray for her?! I'm to talk to her just like I'd do if she'd been in the flock for fifty years—sharing Scripture verses, blessing her comings and goings, esteeming her as a sister in Christ?! Is that it?!

Really, Lord??!! Is that the way I'm supposed to stand in the gap for her?!

OK, Lord. And You want me to read John 4 repeatedly, concerning the way You dealt with an unbeliever? OK, Lord, OK!

[1]Romans 4:18, *KJ*

SQUIRRELLY CHURCH SHOPPERS

Lord Jesus, I intercede for perennial church shoppers who attend worship until someone gets too close—seeking a commitment. Then they move on to another church until they're flushed out once more. Finally they start attending larger churches, so they can blend more inconspicuously into the background of a crowded place—to maintain their anonymity.

I pray for these people. I know that some of them have been hurt by a previous negative church experience, but may they recognize that hiding in ever larger institutional barracks isn't going to equip them to be a good soldier for Jesus Christ.[1]

But then, on the other hand, if they should be captured by enemy forces they'd probably be released quickly because squirrelly non-combatants offer no threat.

[1] 2 Timothy 2:3

CAN YOU BE A CHRISTIAN WITHOUT GOING TO CHURCH?

Lord, for an hour or so I was deeply impressed with the conversation of a successful business-man who belongs to several church organizations and contributes to Christian causes.

Then we went to lunch in his office cafeteria and he told me how he maintained his Christian witness in the business world. Again I was impressed! He let me know about his close association with the local Christian Business-men's Association and his active support of the Mayor's Prayer Breakfast Committee.

When I asked him what local church he belongs to, for a moment he lost his composure. He tried to explain that he was a believer and that's all that mattered—sputter, sputter! But that's not all that matters, is it?

Lord, keep me from judging him.[1] I don't want to be at cross purposes with You; but can a person be a Christian without going to church? Don't we have to have a "body"[2] relationship with brothers and sisters in Christ even though some of them may at times be hard to get along with? Please give me something from Your Word so I can intercede effectively for him—and

[1]Luke 6:37 [2]Ephesians 1:23

accurately speak Your Word to him. Is this what you want me to say? Let us

> . . . not [be] forsaking the assembling of ourselves together, as is the manner of some, but exhorting one another, and so much the more as we see the Day approaching.[3]

I pray in Jesus name that he start assembling as the Day approaches!

[3]Hebrews 10:25, *NKJ*

BIG

Lord, a few of our church leaders keep talking
about us getting big: "The bigger the better."
They say we ought to get big so we can offer
more clout in the community—get more things
done for You.

Lord Jesus, is "big" what You really want—or is
"big" a side issue? I can remember being in a
big church; and often we were guilty of doing
dumb things on a big stage. There's no question
that You want Your church to grow—that's
apparent in Your emphasis on gathering a
harvest[1] and preaching/teaching for decision.[2]
But You also emphasize the importance of the
"few,"[3] the "least,"[4] the "one,"[5] "being alone,"[6]
the "small,"[7] calling someone by his first name,[8]
the body being made up of many parts with no
part, however small, more important than
another.[9] So what should I say to church
leaders obsessed with bigness?

Let me get this down correctly:

> The kingdom of heaven is like a mustard
> seed, which a man took and sowed in his
> field, which indeed is the least of all the seeds:
> but when it is grown it is greater than all the
> herbs and becomes a tree. . . .[10]

[1]John 4:35 [2]Acts 2:14–42 [3]Matthew 22:14 [4]Matthew 25:40
[5]Matthew 18:12–13 [6]John 6:15, *KJ* [7]Mark 12:42
[8]Luke 19:5 [9]1 Corinthians 12:12–25 [10]Matthew 13:31–32,
NKJ 25

Are You saying that we're not to disparage smallness or bigness, that we're to build big people, one person at at time, and those big people will build a big church that'll get blessed?!

Amen, Lord! Amen!

RELIGIOUS CELEBRITY

I pray for him, Lord Jesus. I intercede with tears. He's a religious celebrity. In certain circles he's treated like a king. Even worse, Lord, he's become addicted to all the idolizing. It's gotten to the point now that if he isn't noticed, he's devastated. He's got to be up front or he's peeved. If people don't talk to him *about him* they're perceived as uncaring.

Dear Lord, isn't his egotistic pride just inviting an inevitable fall?[1]

I pray that one day he'll measure the truth of Your words and apply them to his own situation. "No one is good—except God alone."[2] I pray he'll get the message soon! I intercede for all religious "celebs" who wrongly think that what they say or do has any significance beyond Your use of it. May they realize that You and You alone are to be honored first, last, and always.[3]

[1] 1 Timothy 3:6 [2] Luke 18:19 [3] 1 Timothy 1:17

GETTING

Lord God, many people come to worship each Sunday only to get! They worship with out-stretched hands to receive—not all, but many. They come to get a sermon, to get entertaining music, to get a good feeling, to get the Word, to get prayer, to get fellowship. Thankfully most accomplish their mission. But Lord, isn't *getting* just a small part of what worship is supposed to be?

Haven't You told us plainly:

> Therefore, I urge you, brothers, in view of God's mercy, to offer your bodies as living sacrifices, holy and pleasing to God—this is your spiritual act of worship.[1]

I intercede for all us getters who've gotten You into our lives—but who need to understand that we are only part way home.

[1]Romans 12:1

OUT OF UNIFORM

Lord, I intercede with heartfelt sincerity for that
bishop who declared to a national audience that
your Word doesn't fit the specifications of his
intellect. He's worried that bright, sophisticated
people are being turned off by such oddities as
a "three-decker universe" (heaven, earth, hell)
and "demons" that are frequently mentioned on
the pages of Scripture.

Dear God, I'm moved to plead for this brother
and beg You to forgive him for his uninformed
prattle. I pray that tonight he may lift Your
Word from his shelf and turn to Ephesians 6,
allowing the most inspired intellect the church
ever produced to speak directly to his igno-
rance. Maybe he'll notice in the process how
ridiculous a Christian looks out of his uniform
of "armor,"[1] being hung out to dry by unknow-
ing agents of Satan—especially on national
television.

[1]Ephesians 6:13

WHY DO THEY COME?

Lord, I need to intercede for a "new heart . . ."[1] in dealing with those who are forever seeking me out to perform a "Christian funeral" for a non-Christian because he or she was a good person.

Sometimes people totally unrelated to You want to be married in our sanctuary because it's so "pretty," or non-Christian couples stop by to get their children baptized because some member of their family was baptized at our church thirty years ago.

Dear Lord, what is it that causes them to approach us . . . sentiment, tradition, superstition? Or is it You through the power of the Holy Spirit producing a purpose beyond their own, motivating them to come to a place where they can be challenged by Your love as we minister in Your name?[2]

Lord, help me to get over my peevishness in responding to their need. I pray for all us peevish ones who are tempted to withhold what we should share through the opportunities You inspire!

[1]Ezekiel 36:26 [2]1 Thessalonians 1:5

LIFTING THE LOAD

Lord, she left our church staff a few years ago—
feeling unappreciated, unloved, wronged. She
left trailing a mile of angry sparks, denouncing
everyone in sight— more out of hurt than spite.
Frankly, I breathed a sigh of relief when she
left. Later I realized I should have prayed for her
immediately on the spot, without hesitation.
She was carrying a huge load of anger and
confused ill will.

Lord, you've made it very clear that we are to
"bear one another's burdens . . ."[1] regardless of
how we feel about the person or the burden.

I met her the other day with hugs and warm
words, and she told me about a terrible personal disaster. I asked her to come visit with
me, but I didn't pray with her on the spot—and
I should have. Lord, help me to pray even when
I don't want to.

[1]Galatians 6:2, *NKJ*

SNIFFING THE SWEET SAVOR

Lord, I was just reflecting on the assorted difficulties our church has had to overcome during the past few months. At times even the most devout were forced to dip to the bottom of their faith well.

Then in "the fullness of time"[1] You moved on us in a series of blessings, and now we're sniffing the sweet "fragrance"[2] of Your presence.

I can see Your light shining through the faces of those around me—who've prayed us through this testing time. I feel like the Psalmist: "Thou hast beset me behind and before, and laid thine hand upon me."[3]

O Lord, keep Your hand on us—that we may grow not so much in the size of our assembly but in the capacity of our commitment—so we can tackle the major challenges in our community that all but scream for our ministry. I intercede for our congregation—that one day all of us will be able to praise You together:

> Thou art the God that doest wonders: thou hast declared thy strength among the people.[4]

[1]Galatians 4:4 *NKJ* [2]2 Corinthians 2:14 [3]Psalm 139:5, *KJ*
[4]Psalm 77:14, *KJ*

HEARTS TURNED TO STONE

Lord, I intercede for those who're staying away from worship unconsciously. They're like children absent-mindedly playing with their latest toys in an illusory fun-and-games world, not knowing or caring if it's Sunday or Wednesday or when it is. They don't care because they're oblivious to Your reality.

I'm praying for all those who've taken vows of church membership and have subsequently let Satan deceive them into the delusion that worshiping doesn't really matter all that much as long as you've got lots of toys to play with.

I pray for those who, their hearts duped by indulgent neglect, are gradually turning to "stone."[1] Please, Lord, I pray that they be restored with a "heart of flesh."[2]

[1–2]Ezekiel 36:26

THE SHINING ONES

Dear Lord, I'm interceding for Christians who've gotten the uninspired idea that witnessing for You is mostly a formula of rehearsed words, manufactured techniques, quotable sure-shot scriptures!

O Lord, what outrageous nonsense! I pray that potential witnessers—those evangelistically gifted Christians everywhere who've met You, fallen in love with You, and had their lives changed by You—will just allow themselves to do precisely what You've so marvelously ordered:

> Let your light so shine before men, that they may see your good works and glorify your Father in heaven.[1]

Then may it be said of them:

> Those who are wise shall shine like the brightness of the firmament, and those who turn many to righteousness like the stars forever and ever.[2]

Lord, it doesn't take a method to shine—does it?

[1]Matthew 5:16, *NKJ* [2]Daniel 12:3, *NKJ*

34

GOLDEN BOWLS

Lord, I'm interceding tonight for an evangelistic team working in our city prior to a big crusade. They've been emphasizing prayer, the vital place of Your Word,[1] and waiting on the Lord in believing anticipation.[2]

But now they're in a financial crunch and are resorting to a city-wide telephone solicitation, begging for financial help to meet the campaign budget.

Lord, I believe You gave me a picture of how we are to move in such situations—whenever we're being challenged by a lack of funds, or when we're trying to meet other needs in the church. Reading in the Book of Revelation, I saw the "twenty-four elders" gathered around Your throne holding up golden bowls of incense "which are the prayers of the saints."[3] My heart leaped as I was suddenly aware that You're receiving my prayers right now. Then I realized that those in fellowship with You don't have to go around begging the *world* for what *You want.* All we need to do is fill the golden bowls of heaven with intercessory prayers, chase off the Devil, and leave the rest to You.

Dear God, let me at it!

[1] 2 Timothy 3:16, *KJ* [2] Psalm 27:14, *KJ* [3] Revelation 5:8

SIDETRACKED

He's a magnificent church leader—a splendid worker. O Lord, how blessed his church is to have his exceptional talent in their ministry. However, I intercede for him because lately he's gotten sidetracked by carrying a grudge against someone who recently wronged him. Now he's gotten into the bad habit of explaining at great length how absolutely justified he is in being angry.

But Lord, so what if he is right and the other person's wrong? So what? I can't find any place in Your Word where You've called us to win arguments—only to "forgive"[1] and be "reconciled."[2]

Lord, I pray that You can use this prayer to support his love of You in doing what You've told *all* of us Christians to do—with any antagonist.

[1]Mark 11:25–26 [2]Matthew 5:24

BRIGHT IDEAS

Lord, I intercede for our church leadership.
We're into the brainstorming mode again—
trying to come up with bright new ideas to keep
the church hive buzzing.

Help us to "wait on the Lord"[1] however long it
takes, whatever form it takes, whether we like it
or not—so we can have the blessing of Your
counsel.

Lord, we can't make a ministry or ministries
come about anyway, can we?! Isn't it only when
we become aware of what You're doing and
make ourselves available to Your programs and
strategies that things begin to accelerate in the
right direction?

Lord, I pray You can work in and through us as
we watch to see where You're going!

[1]Psalm 37:34, *KJ*

COFFEE HOUR CONVERSATIONS

Lord, I just walked past some friends after church in the Coffee Hour. They were having an animated conversation about their latest golf game and making plans for the next one.

Lord, I stand "in the gap"[1] for these friends—not that they stop talking about their favorite sport, but that they prioritize their time, particularly when in the company of other brothers and sisters in Christ, and especially after worship!

Lord, I don't want to come on as a wet blanket; but when we get together as the body of Christ, shouldn't we at least have something more important to talk about than our golf game? Shouldn't we "speak of the glory of thy kingdom, and talk of thy power"[2] and how to serve the world, especially after worship—ESPECIALLY after worship!!

[1]Ezekiel 22:30, *KJ* [2]Psalm 145:11, *KJ*

SALT AND LIGHT

Lord Jesus, I'm praying for our church confessionally (because I'm part of it) and intercessionally (because I know we can do better).

I'm guilty along with others of criticizing the pagan values of the secular world with a snobbish attitude of pious disgust while doing nothing about it. Please forgive me for avoiding the specifics of Your command to be "salt"[1] and "light"[2] in the world in order to change it.

I pray for a gathering army of zesty and bright activist intercessors from churches all over the world who will purposefully, at a moment's notice, "stand in the gap"[3]—touching the world where they are in Your name,[4] seasoning their culture and brightening the stage where they're located according to Your "will"[5]—beginning today, as we/they make our way through the darkening world You've intended that we light up and season with Your love!

[1]Matthew 5:13, *KJ* [2]Matthew 5:14, *KJ* [3]Ezekiel 22:30, *KJ*
[4]Matthew 18:20 [5]James 4:15

BLESSED

Father, I pray for all my retarded friends at the
group home up the street. One of them called
yesterday to say "good-bye." The home is being
sold. He and his friends must move elsewhere.
He called to say that he "liked coming to our
church"—that he wanted me to pray for him.
Then he said, "God bless you!" Lord, I receive
his blessing . . . made all the more special
because it comes from "one of the least of these
[your] brethren."[1]

I intercede for all those who are as he is, and
for those who care for and esteem them, and for
all who are doing medical research on their
behalf—seeking to improve the quality of their
lives. Mostly though, I pray for him—this one
through whom You chose to bless me.

Thank You, Lord!

[1]Matthew 25:40, *NKJ*

SHE'S ANGRY

Lord, I intercede for her. It's as if she's driven by an obsession to prove her point against another Christian.

Sure, there's an element of truth in what she's saying—but the problem is the poisonously angry way she's saying it.

I pray in Jesus' name that she'll cool off, simmer down, mellow out and start forgiving.[1]

For her own soul's sake, may she learn to pray:

> "O Lord of Hosts, you arc just. See the hearts and motives of these men. Repay them for all that they have planned! I look to you for justice."[2]

[1]Mark 11:25 [2]Jeremiah 11:20, *LB*

"KNOWN IN HELL"

Lord, I was just wondering—when Satan and his demons hold a "Board of Trustees" meeting, do they ever talk about me or discuss what our church is doing and call our church people by name? Are we known in hell?

I got to thinking about this after rereading the story concerning the seven sons of Sceva in the Book of Acts, who, after watching Paul cast out demons by the name of Jesus, decided to imitate his method—probably for profit. So after listening to Paul's words spoken through the sons of Sceva, the demon in the guy declared: "Jesus I know, and I know about Paul, but who are you?"[1] And with that the demon-possessed man jumped on the seven sons and beat them to a bloody pulp.

Lord, it's wonderful that we're known in heaven—that You know us as Your followers—that even the angels know us; but shouldn't we also be known in hell like it is with Jesus and Paul?

I pray that as we become a growing threat to Satan by stealing his converts, wrecking his sin machinery, tearing down his idols, we'll have identity recognition not only in heaven but also in hell.

[1]Acts 19:15

42

CHAPTER 11

Dear Lord, I'm interceding for a friend who came to our church several years ago. He joined our fellowship and was faithful in Bible study and worship. He became a member of the Board of Deacons, and on one occasion preached for me. However, as long as I've known him, he's had an all-consuming obsession to be financially independent; more than that—to become enormously wealthy. If only I'd been able to challenge his ambition in light of Your Word:

> People who want to get rich fall into temptation and a trap and into many foolish and harmful desires that plunge men into ruin and destruction. For the love of money is a root of all kinds of evil. Some people, eager for money, have wandered from the faith and pierced themselves with many griefs.[1]

Ten years ago he quit coming to church—too busy making money. Now he's under indictment on varying charges of fraud, and today he declared bankruptcy. I'm sick at heart for him as he's being pierced with many griefs. I pray for him with sobs of compassion.[2] I struggle in intercession that he will come to You as his only master, repent of his sins, receive You as "Lord and Savior,"[3] and finally realize the truth of Your word, "What good is it for a man to gain the whole world, and yet lose or forfeit his very self?"[4]

[1] 1 Timothy 6:9-10 [2] Romans 12:15 [3] 2 Peter 3:18 [4] Mark 8:36, *paraphrased*

PRAYING FOR THE INDIVIDUAL

ON FLIGHT 223

Lord, I praise You for that intercessor who got up from her seat and walked down the aisle of a crowded plane. Attractively dressed, with precise bearing, she stopped beside a mother with two sick kids who were alternately throwing up, with temperatures of 102 degrees. In full view of scores of travelers she asked very politely but firmly, "May I pray for you?" which she did, in Your "name."[1] Lovingly she lifted the "little children of God,"[2] as she called them, to Your healing care. And amazingly those "beloved"[3] little ones fell asleep for two and a half hours.

After praying, the intercessor quietly went back to her seat as though nothing had happened . . . NOTHING—except a powerful demonstration of Your unconditional love flowing through a pray-er ready to stand "in the gap."[4]

Lord, I want to "go and do likewise."[5]

[1]John 14:13   [2]Luke 18:16   [3]Psalm 127:2, *KJ*   [4]Ezekiel 22:30, *KJ*   [5]Luke 10:37

PRAYING AND DOING

Lord, don't You want me, as an intercessor, to be praying "hands on" whenever possible? Isn't that what You're saying in Your Word:

Praying for the "hungry"[1] while providing them food.

Praying for the "thirsty"[2] while giving them a drink of water.

Praying for the "stranger"[3] after inviting him/her in for a visit.

Praying for those "needing clothes"[4] and opening my closet.

Praying for the "sick"[5] while holding their hands.

Praying for those "in prison"[6] in the prison visitor's room.

Lord, of course I'll intercede at a distance; but I'm available for person-to-person intercession too—for all the "least of these"[7] You love.

[1-3]Matthew 25:35 [4-6]Matthew 25:36 [7]Matthew 25:40

FITTED TO SERVE

Lord, He came to see me—a jangled, throbbing storm of emotion. He was angry, but fearing his anger might kill him. He is a wealthy man but poor in cash flow. He's a moral man outraged by immorality surfacing in his office. He's a good man, wondering why You've mistreated him through a succession of business failures, turnarounds, and misfortunes. He's shaken, but resolved to get his life back on track.

At first I thought he was under Satanic attack, but then I caught a vision.[1] I saw Your hand on him—chastening,[2] rebuking,[3] humbling,[4] breaking,[5] wounding,[6] sucking the wind out of his sails—causing him to lean[7] on You and You alone.

I stand "in the intercessory gap" for this man, believing he will soon join our company of believers and intercessors. I see him leading others to Christ, ministering in the church.

I give thanks for the opportunity that is his and ours in his coming "to the kingdom for such a time as this."[8] Praise the Lord!

---

[1]Proverbs 29:18, *KJ* [2]Hebrews 12:6, *KJ* Revelation 3:19
[4]Isaiah 5:15 [5]Job 41:25, *KJ* [6]Job 5:18 [7]Proverbs 3:5
[8]Esther 4:14

RAPED

Lord, she came to see me the day after she'd been raped.

She recounted in vivid detail the stalking presence of the one who did it. I tried to console her—my precious sister in Christ—and now I'm interceding for her with a compassion[1] beyond my power to express. Lord, Your Word leaves little room for her to do anything else but forgive;[2] *but it's so hard!!*

Are You saying that the reason she must forgive is to speed the process of forgetting?[3] Is forgiving the means by which we're released from the slavery of flashback remembrance?

I pray that she be strengthened to forgive so that she can redemptively forget! And I pray for the rapist, that he never be able to forget until (God have mercy on his soul) he comes to You seeking forgiveness.

[1]Luke 7:13 [2]Colossians 3:13 [3]Philippians 3:13

INTERCESSION FAILURES

Lord, I'm praying for failed intercessors every-where, including myself.

The other day I shared with a group my recent failure to stand in the gap.[1] I was telling them about the glorious opportunity You gave me to pray for several sports celebrities whom I'd met prior to a major sports award banquet where I was to give the invocation.

> A prominent national sportscaster shared a touching story with me concerning a friend of his in need.
> *I said and did nothing.*
> A baseball manager confided his anxiety at speaking to a large crowd.
> *I said and did nothing.*
> A great singer showed me her nervous, sweaty palms.
> *I said and did nothing.*
> An All-American football player confessed disturbance at the awards system.
> *I said and did nothing.*

Now I realize that Satan struck me with a case of momentary amnesia. I'd forgotten who I am and who I belong to. Thank You for dealing with me all the way home—restoring my sense of identity and reminding me:

> . . . what's the use of saying that you have

[1]Ezekiel 22:30, *KJ*

faith and are Christians if you aren't proving
it by helping others?[2]

After telling this story I asked if anyone in the
group had failed that miserably in their prayer
ministry, and all admitted they had. I intercede
now for *all of us!* Please give us another chance
to ". . . present [our] bodies a living sacrifice,
holy, acceptable, unto [You], which is [our]
reasonable service."[3]

[2]James 2:14, *LB* [3]Romans 12:1, *KJ*

BEWITCHED

Lord Jesus, I'm praying for a writer friend of thirty years. Long ago he was "born again,"[1] saved, committing himself to Your cause without reservation. He became a man of Your Word. His words reflected Your words: "redemption from sin," "salvation," "Jesus' sacrificial blood shed on the cross for our sins," "prayer," "healing," "discipleship in the body of Christ," "judgment."

The other day I read one of his latest writings—actually not his but those of one he calls his "spirit guide"—sprinkled with the vocabulary of the new age: "energies," "mother earth," "union," "ethereal," "awareness," "realization," etc.

Lord, I know how easy it is to become "bewitched"[2] by the counterfeiting fraud of Satan. Somehow my friend's gotten out from under the authority of Your Word, leaving him unprotected without spiritual armor.[3] Even worse, he's blinded to the insidious way the "adversary"[4] will disguise himself as "an angel of light,"[5] even a spirit guide ("familiar spirit"),[6] then move in "to steal and kill and destroy."[7] I pray for my friend with anguished tears, that he repent from his prodigal detour and return to the foot of the cross and his roots in You.

[1]John 3:7 [2]Galatians 3:1 [3]Ephesians 6:11 [4]1 Peter 5:8, *KJ*
[5]2 Corinthians 11:14 [6]Leviticus 20:21, *KJ* [7]John 10:10

NUMBER ONE

He was once a great athlete, Lord, and now he's
a Christian. But he's still trying to be number
one—the star, the acclaimed all-Christian, the
main man. Even in the "body of Christ"[1] he
keeps trying to outdo anyone who would com-
pete with him as "the" acknowledged leader.

I intercede passionately for him. In the name of
Jesus, I bind back that prideful[2] spirit of com-
petitiveness that's been cutting him off from
fellowship not only in the church but with
members of his own family. I pray believingly[3]
for his deliverance from this bondage that's
prevented him from being what he is in You, a
selfless, loving man, submitted to his family,
friends, brothers and sisters in the church,
unconcerned about whether he's number one or
one thousand.

[1] 1 Corinthians 12:27   [2] Proverbs 16:18   [3] Matthew 21:22,
NKJ

GOING TO HELL

Lord, You'd think she'd get the message after years of making everyone around her miserable—mostly because she's never been able to forgive her sister who did something to her fifty years ago. She's suffering everything from shingles to blindness.

Her skin's chewed up with the scourge of anxiety. Her revengeful eyes blink—seeing less and less. She's been warned repeatedly that if she's ever to escape from the prison of ill health she must stop saying nasty things about her sister and "forgive,"[1] whatever the offense. Lord, I'm interceding for more than her health. It's her soul I'm concerned about! I'm praying that she "repent,"[2] stop violating God's will for her life, and forgive—or she'll be plunged into a place where there's no forgiveness . . . ever.[3]

[1]Matthew 10:35 [2]Acts 17:30 [3]Matthew 5:22

BEING DUMPED ON

Lord Jesus, I'm interceding for a man who's been telling me about all the bad stuff "being dumped on him."

He said, "I'm trying to live a godly life but terrible things keep happening."

Then I remembered the story You told concerning certain Jews who reported to You about Governor Pontius Pilate carrying off a successful assassination plot against some protestors from Galilee.[1] The Jews pressed You to agree that this was a terrible atrocity against godly people. Instead You told them to repent,[2] explaining that just being on the side of right doesn't necessarily make *you* right.

Lord, help me to tell this "dumped on" man that he needs to repent—right, wrong, or indifferent—and turn his life totally over to You. May he accept being cut down to size, taken apart, pruned, chastened,[3] even "crucified with Christ."[4] I pray he be reassembled in You and sent on his journey, perhaps traveling the same general direction but on a different route and with a new traveling companion, walking now in "newness of life"[5] and no longer just trying to be good!

[1]Luke 13:1 [2]Luke 13:5 [3]Hebrews 12:5–11 [4]Galatians 2:20
[5]Romans 6:4, *KJ*

FOR JIM

Lord, today I'm having an "in the body of Christ"[1] experience. This one's painful. As You've said, when ". . . one member suffers, all suffer together."[2]

I'm interceding with tears for an unfulfilled friend. He's loaded with talent but for some reason he's in a no-win blind-alley employment situation. He's going nowhere vocationally and becoming sadly resigned to the career in which he's trapped.

I feel You urging me to "bear"[3] (to lift) him from his "infirmities"[4] (his present way of thinking about himself) in prayer right now ! In fact, Lord, I'm going to pray his name into an intercessory prayer You inspired through St. Paul:

> I pray that Jim ". . . be strengthened with might through [Your] Spirit in the inner man, that Christ may dwell in [Jim's] heart through faith; that [he], being rooted and grounded in love, may be able to comprehend with all the saints what is the width and length and depth and height—to know the love of Christ which passes knowledge; that [Jim] may be filled with all the fullness of God."[5]

[1]1 Corinthians 12:27 [2]1 Corinthians 12:26, *RS* [3]Romans 15:1, *KJ* [4]Romans 15:1, *KJ* [5]Ephesians 3:16–19, *NKJ*

HEART AS WELL AS MIND

Lord Jesus, He insists that he wants to know You. I pray his towering, highly prized intellect won't get in the way.

I ask that he may follow the exact dictate of Your Word and learn to exercise the full capacity of his heart in faith:

> And you will seek Me and find Me, when you search for Me with all your heart.[1]

I also pray he pay close attention to Job:

> Canst thou by searching find out God?[2]

Aren't You saying here that not even the brightest minds can do this?

> For as the heavens are higher than the earth, so are my ways higher than your ways, and my thoughts than your thoughts.[3]

O Lord, I pray he will come to know You with all his heart as well as all his mind so that his connection with You will transcend merely collecting theological information.

May he come to know You as his loving personal friend,[4] Lord and Savior,[5] as well as his transcendent "King of glory."[6]

---

[1]Jeremiah 29:13, *NKJ* [2]Job 11:7, *KJ* [3]Isaiah 55:9, *KJ*
[4]John 15:15 [5]2 Peter 3:18 [6]Psalm 24:7

NEW ORDERS

Lord Jesus, one thing that's happened since I got into this intercessory business is that I've had to change not only my way of praying, but my way of thinking about people.

Here I am praying by name for murderers, prostitutes, druggers, gamblers, con artists, thieves, liars, etc., in my Alcoholics Anonymous 5th step work. I've had to learn not to consider the person's outward circumstances but just aim to get him to You as soon as possible. In the process, You've put me under different orders with a radical new calling: "A new commandment I give to you, that you love one another; as I have loved you, that you also love one another."[1]

Lord, keep me submissive to the law of Your love—the same law that got You nailed to the cross for me and all those I'm praying for.

[1] John 13:34, *NKJ*

MATURING

Lord, I'm pleading for a brother in Christ—a new Christian, a new churchman. He's a wonderfully successful businessman. Now he's received You into his life and it's been wonderful to behold. However, I'm noticing that he's practicing some of the same attitudes in the church that he exerts in the business world. He's trying to control. He's attempting to take charge. There's not much "yield"[1] in him; and even worse, he's trying to make himself look good.

O Lord, I pray he come to recognize what he's doing—that he's actually setting himself up against You: "God resists the proud. . . ."[2] May he see he's in a no-win situation. Please, Lord, I pray he will mature in the faith slowly but surely, hearing You speak to him through St. Paul:

> Not that I have already obtained this or am already perfect; but I press on to make it my own, because Christ Jesus has made me his own. Brethren, I do not consider that I have made it my own; but one thing I do, forgetting what lies behind . . . I press on toward the goal for the prize of the upward call of God in Christ Jesus. Let those of us who are mature be thus minded. . . . [3]

Amen!

[1]Romans 6:13, *KJ* [2]James 4:6, *NKJ* [3]Philippians 3:12–15, *RS*

HURTING

My Lord and my God, tonight I pray with passion and compassion for a dear man who underwent quadruple-bypass heart surgery plus a valve replacement two days ago. Now he's suffering from unexpected complications.

I pray as Elijah did, with my face between my knees.[1] Even as a mother birthing a child leans into her contractions, so I'm praying for this man that he be birthed from his pain. I beseech You to relax the tensions for his trauma, that You touch[2] his throbbing wounds, and that he shall hear You say in the swirling storm of his painful, dark night, "Peace, be still."[3] May he catch sight of Your "light"[4] along the shore of his suffering. Tonight, please lead him to a safe, peaceful harbor where he can rest from his ordeal.

[1] 1 Kings 18:42 [2] Mark 10:13 [3] Mark 4:39, *KJ* [4] 1 John 1:5

WHO *IS* WHO?

Lord, I've just had my second encounter with
a woman who comes on so strongly that she's
gotten the reputation of leaving destruction in
her wake. It's like she has to contend—exhibit-
ing varying degrees of hostility just to be noticed.

Frankly, I've avoided praying for her though
I know I should. However, in our latest go-
around I saw a drive, a force, an attempt to
dominate, boiling out of her that could only
have originated in hell. Suddenly I realized
who it is I've been dealing with. Quick—let me
make sure I've got my prayer armor on. All at
once I realize I'm not wrestling against "flesh
and blood"—certainly not that poor mixed-up
woman across from me. I'm struggling against
"the rulers of the darkness of this world"[1] who
are stoking her aggressiveness.

[1]Ephesians 6:12, *KJ*

PRUNING

Lord, I intercede for that extraordinarily talented man who was just passed over for top management in his company. Now he's fighting the gut-wrenching temptation to lash out at those who've been evaluating him, judging him, denying him, and attempting to box him in.

I pray in his place, knowing that he's hurting too much to come to You just now. I pray that before his disappointment turns to self-pity and bitterness he will catch a fresh revelation of what You endured in the flesh. How You were repeatedly turned down, passed over, ignored, "rejected."[1] I pray that soon he'll let Your servant Paul's healing words minister to him:

> We are hard pressed on every side, yet not crushed; we are perplexed, but not in despair; persecuted, but not forsaken; struck down, but not destroyed—always carrying about in the body the dying of the Lord Jesus, that the life of Jesus also may be manifested in our body.[2]

I pray that one day he'll look back on this shattering experience in January from the perspective of grace—seeing it as merely a midwinter pruning to produce a better crop in the spring.

[1] 1 Peter 2:4 [2] 2 Corinthians 4:8–10, *NKJ*

MORE THAN CONVERSION

Lord, I'm interceding for a man who's been making a mess of his life. He used to come to church. Now he's gone. When he was asked to rejoin us, he affected the veneer of arrogance with a "who cares" attitude.

Lord, he's lost—and tonight I feel lost for him as I "travail"[1] in tears for his redemption from sin. I'm not praying that he just get converted—he needs more than that. I pray he be "born again"[2] all over again.

Lord, You've supplied all his needs with grace beyond grace. You've shed Your blood for him! You've gotten the gospel to him! Your light has shined upon him! But it appears that Satan, "the god of this world,"[3] has blinded him. I say now—in the name of the Lord Jesus Christ— that the power of Satan be broken in this man. I claim his deliverance from the darkness of self-delusion and call him out of the tomb of death.

[1]Galatians 4:19, *KJ* [2]John 3:3 [3]2 Corinthians 4:4, *KJ*

UPTIGHT SAINT

Lord, I'm interceding for a "saint."[1] She's dedicated, committed, devoted, faithful. She's also earnest to the point of tears, devoutly grim, piously humorless, cringingly consecrated.

She didn't start out that way! She used to celebrate You spontaneously, jubilantly ! Now all that's changed. She's into theological doctrine, religious tradition, rules, regulations, inflexible devotional discipline, oughtness, and constant uptightness over "whether or not I'm doing it right."

I pray she please stop close-step marching long enough to listen to You:

> I have come that they may have life, and that they may have it more abundantly.[2]

> These things I have spoken to you, that My joy may remain in you, and that your joy may be full.[3]

Lord, I pray that she unclench her white knuckles, loosen her set jaw and taut muscles, relax her shallow breathing, so she can just be at peace with You and enjoy the pleasure of Your company.

[1]Philippians 4:21 [2]John 10:10, *NKJ* [3]John 15:11, *NKJ*

ON HER CASE

Lord, I intercede for this woman who's desperately struggling with what she should do with her life. She's failed so many times with undirected shots in the dark. She identifies herself as a rebel—having rejected authority most of her life. Her favorite expression is, "Get off my case!"

But isn't authority what she needs more than anything else, along with someone who will redemptively work on her case and compassionately direct her way? Above all she needs You, Lord, saying strongly to her:

"This is the way, walk in it."[1]

I pray intercessionally for her that she repent of her stubborn willfulness, be cleansed of the fear of committing her life to You, and finally submit herself into Your transforming, redirecting hands.

[1]Isaiah 30:21, *NKJ*

MIRACLE

Lord, I'm interceding for a Christian sister 3,000 miles away. Physically she's afflicted by cancer, but her spirit is strong. Her testimony has never once diminished. But she's been going through the classic stages of deterioration. Then two weeks ago a new wonder drug came on the market. Tests were made to see if she could be a candidate for the drug—and she is.

Lord, is this the breakthrough we've been praying for? We'll take it any way You give it. We're standing in agreement[1] that this "saint"[2] not leave us just yet—that a "miracle"[3] be allowed for the upbuilding of many. May we all hear You say loud and clear, "Behold, I am the Lord, the God of all flesh: is there any thing too hard for me?"[4]

No, Lord, no!

[1]Matthew 18:19 [2]Acts 9:32 [3]John 12:18, *KJ* [4]Jeremiah 32:27, *KJ*

HELP

Lord, I've been interceding for this problem-plagued man for a long time and nothing seems to HELP. But yesterday a word from Your Word got magnified ten sizes. I was reading, "Likewise the Spirit also HELPS in our weaknesses. For we do not know what we should pray for as we ought, but the Spirit Himself makes intercession for us with groanings which cannot be uttered."[1]

Then I was out at the Air Force Base watching my navigator son-in-law taking off in his RF4 fighter plane. I watched him soar upward—23,000 feet in 40 seconds. But he couldn't have done it without the HELP of his pilot and a two-man ground crew.

Dear Lord, in the person of the Holy Spirit You are with me right now as "The HELPER."[2] You are HELPING me intercede for this man. You won't do my interceding for me—but You're here to HELP.

Praise God—let's do it!

[1]Romans 8:26, *NKJ* [2]John 14:26, *NKJ*

LORD OF ALL THINGS

Lord, it happened in a "share-prayer" group the other night. I love this group—and all those in the other groups too! They are my spiritual family!

I praise You for allowing us to share such wonderful closeness with each other and especially with You. But on this particular evening the bottom fell out. We were confessing so many hurts, disruptions, problems, crises, that I could actually feel the presence of evil attacking the walls of our faith cathedral.

Suddenly I remembered Paul's letter to the church at Ephesus. He was writing to people under siege—assaulted by the relentless pounding of Satan. He prayed for that church—that they be given "the spirit of wisdom and revelation in the knowledge of Him" and that "the eyes of [their] understanding [be] enlightened," so that they would know the "exceeding greatness of [God's] power . . . which He worked in Christ when He raised Him from the dead, . . . far above all principality and power and might and dominion . . . and put all things under His feet. . . ."[1]

Dear God, what a prayer! It's like You chal-

[1]Ephesians 1:17–23, *NKJ*

longed those early Christians to make a choice—deliberately to choose good over evil, hope over despair, life over death; and to live like Jesus really is Lord, not just of the church but over "all things," including the enemy hammering away out there in the dark.

LIKE DAVID

Lord, the other day I was thinking (that's where I made my first mistake) about the size of our intercessory group.

We're "small,"[1] "weak,"[2] "lowly,"[3] "foolish,"[4] having only begun. Yet You keep calling us to astounding tasks and sometimes I wonder if You've counted our numbers recently.

A friend just told me about a meeting he had with a famous football coach whose team was about to play in a nationally telecast game.

The coach asked my friend, "Do you read the Bible?" He answered, "Yes." "Did you ever read the story of David and Goliath?" My friend said, "Yes." The coach said, "Well, our team is David and they're Goliath."

Lord, wasn't he saying that David won the contest with Goliath *not* because of his size, power, stature, or reputation—but by his faith and that alone?

Amen, Lord, we'll remain Your understaffed minority standing "in the gap." BUT THE REST IS UP TO YOU.

[1]Isaiah 60:22 [2]2 Corinthians 13:4–9 [3]Proverbs 16:19
[4]1 Corinthians 1:27

PRAYING FOR THE FAMILY

OUR

Lord, I know they've been married for twelve years, but are they really married? I intercede for them not just because they're Christians but because they don't know how to be Christians in marriage. They say they want a 50-50 marriage—which is about the percentage each is giving the other.

He calls her "the wife." She calls him "old Dad." Their son is "her boy." Their daughter is "his girl." The house is "hers." The yard is "his." One car is "his," the other is "hers." He's got "his" job and she's got "hers." It's "his money" and "her money." The church is "hers." The club is "his."

I pray in Jesus name that next time they pray the Lord's prayer they pray only the first word "Our"[1] and then apply it to everything they call "his" or "hers"—making it "our kids," "our house," "our yard," "our cars," "our jobs," "our money," "our church," "our club," and most certainly ". . . our Lord Jesus Christ."[2]

[1]Matthew 6:9 [2]2 Peter 1:8

I'LL TAKE NATALIE ANY DAY

Lord, I pray for that unhappy couple whose faces seem set in a perpetual smile. They're so incredibly bored with each other, packaged like two dead fish in a flimsy wrapping they call marriage. They were deceived into thinking that compatibility is the essence of a solid relationship. They're so much alike they make each other sick!

O Lord, I pray that the unique personhood You once put in them will surface so that they'll have a saving explosion of dynamic interaction, coming out from behind their masks, and letting the chips fall where they may!

By contrast, thank you, dear Lord, for my wife, Natalie, my exact opposite, who rips into me— then heals; who scolds—then loves; who criticizes—then praises.

> The heart of her husband trusts in her, and he will have no lack of gain. She does him good, and not harm, all the days of her life.[1]

[1]Proverbs 31:11–12, *RS*

EMOTIONAL DIVORCE

Lord Jesus, I pray for those two friends who think they're married because they've lived together for thirty years. He goes out with his buddies: golfing, poker playing, to business luncheons, the club, on weekend fishing trips.

She's out and about too—with her friends: playing tennis, shopping, lunching, at bridge games. Now and then they come to church together. The truth is they're living separate lives, yet pretending not to.

For some time he's been telling his buddies the secret issues of his heart—things he used to tell her. And she does the same—sharing with others what once was their personal pillow talk. Somewhere they lost vital communication, not ". . . speaking the truth in love."[1] I pray that one day they will finally decide to do something together—like meet at the foot of the cross and be "washed" together in Your blood—for forgiveness of their marriage sins.[2]

[1]Ephesians 4:15 [2]Ephesians 5:25

TRYING TOO HARD

Lord God, I want to intercede for so many who feel guilty about their job of parenting—myself included.

When I read scriptures like, "Fathers, do not exasperate your children; instead, bring them up in the training and instruction of the Lord,"[1] I feel like a failure, because while our kids have confessed You as Lord, they're far from being as perfect as I think they should be.

It just occurred to me—You've had some problems along that line too. In fact, You lost all Your kids to sin except One—and even His closest disciples at one point deserted Him.

Lord, are You telling me to pray confidently for all those who're doing their loving best in Christ for their sons and daughters, recognizing that love "bears all things, believes all things, hopes all things, endures all things. . ."?[2] And the two best things we can do for our kids are to (1) quit trying so hard and (2) quit feeling guilty—both of which suffocate the joyously creative love You gave us when we became parents? Lord, please help us do what's necessary to restore the joy!

[1]Ephesians 6:4 [2]1 Corinthians 13:7, *NKJ*

SECOND THOUGHTS

Lord, for a year or so she thought he'd be the one with whom she'd share her life. They'd marry, establish a home, have children, build a business, and grow old together. Now she's having second thoughts! And it all has to do with You!

He's a traditionalist Christian. She's a radical one. He's religiously oriented. She's got a personal relationship with You. He's tolerant of her views. She's demanding his total commitment to You! He sees marriage as a good institution. She sees it as a spiritual union.

I pray for these two—who really are two—that they may recognize their "twoness" and for the time being go their separate ways. I pray for him, that he "repent, and believe in the gospel"[1] that she's been trying to open to him; so that if it is Your will that they rejoin, they'll most certainly become "one."[2] I pray that day will come!

[1]Mark 1:15, *NKJ* [2]Matthew 19:6

BLAST ME, LORD

Lord, I've not even come close to being an adequate intercessor—particularly for my own family. I try to remember my covenant to pray daily for each member of our clan, but some days I forget. And when nighttime comes, I'm so weary I can't pray.

I keep failing those who need my prayers—and You, who await my standing in the gap[1] on behalf of someone. "What a wretched man I am!"[2] Lord, You have every right to blast me with words of purging condemnation lashing out at my sinful lack of discipline. I've got the Bible open, I'm ready—I think! So here goes:

> But He, being full of compassion, forgave their iniquity, and did not destroy them. Yes, many a time He turned His anger away, and did not stir up all His wrath; for He remembered that they were but flesh, a breath that passes away and does not come again.[3]

Thank you, Lord. I needed that!

[1]Ezekiel 22:30, *KJ* [2]Romans 7:24 [3]Psalm 78:38–39, *NKJ*

WHERE YOUR TREASURE IS

Lord, I'm interceding for that new family in our church. They've got the look of having made it big in the world. It's the excessive, over-ripe smell of success: luxury, comfort, convenience, status—but not much love!

O Lord, I pray that one day soon they'll hear You say: "Do not store up for yourselves treasure on earth, where moth and rust destroy, and where thieves break in and steal."[1] I pray they'll be released from stuff that has to be possessed, guarded, taken care of to the point of anxious obsession.

Let them invest in the ministry of people, where You honor the gift and bless the giver with "treasures in heaven"[2] that pay off in pure joy and the sweet fragrance of Your loving presence—that doesn't have to be locked up!

[1]Matthew 6:19 [2]Matthew 6:20

AS

Lord, he's a big, tough, macho husband nominally related to You, who keeps reminding his Christian wife to submit[1] to him. He rules his roost with the authority of brute strength. He's the king—only she isn't the queen; in fact, she's the unpaid help.

I intercede for both of these misguided people. First for the husband—that he put on his bifocals the next time he reads Ephesians 5:

> Husbands, love your wives, just as Christ loved the church and gave himself up for her. . . .[2]

Lord, aren't You saying that a husband is to love his wife in the same way that Christ gave Himself for us on the cross—that is, sacrificially? Doesn't "as" mean that a husband should be sacrificially giving himself to grocery shopping, getting up with sick kids, doing the dishes, changing diapers, cleaning the house, staying home so his wife can go out, listening to her when she speaks, treasuring her mind and spirit as well as her body, praying with her, ministering to her—putting her feelings first?

[1]Ephesians 5:22 [2]Ephesians 5:25

CALL IN THE ANGELS

Lord, often when praying for my family members scattered around the country I call for angels to help me; in fact, I've even given orders for angelic assistance like it was my right. Someone once told me to do that—but now I find it's contrary to Your Word.

I have no business ordering Your angels to do anything, least of all to protect my loved ones. Forgive me, Lord, for listening to people instead of clearing it through Your Word:

> For *He* shall give His angels charge over you,
> to keep you in all your ways.[1]

Lord, they're *Your* angels, and *You're* the only one who can rightly order them to do anything. So tonight I pray that You will please send a bunch of them to do some "ministering"[2] to every member of my family because they need all the help You can give them.

[1]Psalm 91:11, *NKJ* [2]Hebrews 1:14

SOUL KNOWLEDGE

Lord, I pray for the youngest daughter in that family. Her parents are always comparing her with her "brilliant" older sister. Her parents know better, but they keep doing it. When report cards come home, they're opened at the dinner table in front of everyone. The youngest always ends up looking terrible by comparison.

I pray that younger sister may find a new support system, beginning with her relationship with You, so that she'll find reassurance in Your Word as to how valuable she really is, and from time to time reflect on who and what she is according to Your Word:

> I will praise You, for I am fearfully and wonderfully made; marvelous are Your works, and that my soul knows very well.[1]

[1]Psalm 139:14, *NKJ*

FOR WIDOWS

Lord, I pray for women in our church stricken
by the death of their husbands—grieving sometimes for months. I've seen their tears flowing
at the sight of his old hat, his Bible, the dog
with no walking companion, an empty chair at
the table . . . Christmas, Thanksgiving, birth-
days, alone.

I pray You will remind me on my daily rounds
to "visit"[1] them, "defend"[2] and "protect"[3] them.
I intercede for them in prayer that they receive
sustaining spiritual comfort by Your Holy
Spirit . . . that they give Satan no place by
self-indulgence. I pray that they take to heart
Your word about the benefits of the cross:
"Surely he hath borne our griefs, and carried
our sorrows. . . ."[4]

By the way—I pray for widowers too, who need
the same ministering.

[1]James 1:27, *KJ* [2]Isaiah 1:17 [3]Jeremiah 22:3, *LB*
[4]Isaiah 53:4, *KJ*

EMPTY NEST

Lord, their kids are grown and gone. The two of them are left in a rambling old house built for six. They're terribly bored, lonely, rattling around with nothing to do in their present state of terminal retirement.

I intercede for them that they take on a new project, like building something together—designating You as the head architect, building superintendent, master carpenter, plumber, electrician, painter, designer, outfitter from top to bottom. For "unless the Lord builds the house, its builders labor in vain."[1]

In that newly created place, I pray they learn to pray and read the Bible together daily, and witness for You wherever they go—even in Hawaii. May they give their tithe not only to the church, but also to Christ-centered missionary work. And then follow up—even to driving a pick-up truck to haul left-over food from stores and bakeries to the food bank, staying long enough to help share it with others—specifically *not* just at Thanksgiving and Christmas.

Praise God, I see them doing it!

[1]Psalm 127:1

PRAYING FOR THE WORLD

DOWN GO THE IDOLS

Lord, sometimes when I consider the enormous
problems of our world I feel hopelessly small
and insignificant. These problems, that even
governments seem unable to solve, are like
great icons of secular tragedy that we tiptoe by
in silent fear and awe. We are all but worshiping our multi-megaton problems.

I felt Your nudge to read again 1 Samuel 5,
which tells about the time the Ark of the Covenant was captured by the Philistines and
taken into the same house where their idol god,
Dagon, was on display. The next morning they
found "Dagon, fallen on his face . . . before the
ark of the Lord."[1] They set Dagon back on his
feet but, alas, the following morning the same
thing happened—only this time Dagon's head
and hands were severed from his torso. So the
Philistine priests wisely decided to return the
ark to Israel.

The truth is that in Your presence the Dagons
of this world inevitably fall.

Praise God! Are You saying that in a world
wobbling along worshiping so many monstrous
problems, I'm to seek to introduce You into
every problem situation—and that in so doing I

[1]1 Samuel 5:3

bring Your presence into the idol's house? Then it's just a matter of time until somehow, one day Dagon will fall!

Praise the Lord!

POLLUTING A PLANET

Lord, I'm interceding for our planet. I'm standing in an ever-widening gap against a rampag-
ing current of slimy pollution surging across
our TV/movie screens.

It's like a group of film producers, infected with
a terminal disease of "lust"[1] with accompanying
lascivious[2] fantasies and obsessions, are deter-
mined to infect the entire world with their
epidemic sickness. The other night I sat down
to watch what critics were calling "the best
television has to offer—something truly remark-
able." I remember one captivating scene, magnificently scripted, beautifully acted, perfectly
directed, gorgeously photographed, with only
one observable flaw—the subject matter was
absolutely forbidden by Your Word.[3] It all
looked so innocent, so honest, so open-faced
and natural—only it orginated from the "pit,"[4]
and its intent is to ". . . steal and kill and
destroy."[5] Lord, we're under attack! The moral
fibre of our nation and our world is threatened.
Inspire us to "put on the whole armor of God,
that [we] may be able to stand against the wiles
of the devil."[6]

[1] John 2:16, *KJ* [2] 1 Peter 4:3, *KJ* [3] 1 Corinthians 6:15–16
[4] Revelation 20:3, *KJ* [5] John 10:10 [6] Ephesians 6:11, *NKJ*

MARVELOUS MARVIN

Lord, he says he's retired—but he's become our town's most prolific gatherer of recyclable material. Day and night he's out in his old VW van picking up other people's newspapers, cardboard boxes, bottles, aluminum cans and other stuff. He hauls his mountain of trash—tied with a rope, and sometimes twice as high as his vehicle—off to a recycling center. He knows the odds against making a major ecological impact are enormous, but long ago he decided to make a difference, personally. He decided to take responsible "dominion"[1] and to faithfully "subdue"[2] his part of the earth in all its critical need.

Praise God for Marvin! As he collects newspapers he's well aware of the awesome statistic that if every human being on earth bought a newspaper each day, all the forests would be destroyed in 30 years. So he's volunteering to "stand in the gap" on behalf of the rest of us newspaper junkies—to slow down the ravage of our forests through his commitment to recycling.

Thank you, Lord, for this man with a cause—a doer of the Word and not a hearer only.[3] He's challenging us and we need it! I intercede for him for strengthening, and us for awareness.

[1]Genesis 1:28, *KJ* [2]Genesis 1:28, *KJ* [3]James 1:22, *KJ*

HAVE MERCY ON US, O LORD . . .

She strolled into a local cathedral wearing skins
of animals that are rapidly becoming extinct.
"Have mercy on us, O Lord . . ."[1]

I watched the homeless in our nation's capital
in soup lines, warming themselves by sidewalk
air grates, staring incredulously at the multi-
million-dollar gala event celebrating the inaugu-
ration of our new President.
"Have mercy on us, O Lord . . ."[2]

I witnessed TV reports of the indiscriminate
bulldozing of vegetation in a South American
country—some of which may contain an organic
substance that could successfully treat an
incurable disease.
"Have mercy on us, O Lord . . ."[3]

I read about debt-ridden countries in Central
America trashing their forests, setting up cattle
ranches to supply beef to American fast food
chains.
"Have mercy on us, O Lord . . ."[4]

The other day the county sent a crew to clean
up a highway oil spill not far from where we
live. They dumped the leftover residue in the
middle of a shallow pit, and may easily have

[1-4]Matthew 20:30, *KJ*

contaminated all the wells in our area.
"Have mercy on us, O Lord . . ."[5]

One of the factories in our city insists that it is
in compliance with the clean air act—by now
having draped a burlap sack over its smoke-
stack.
"Have mercy on us, O Lord . . ."[6]

[5-6]Matthew 20.30, *KJ*

WALT'S FRUSTRATION

Lord, I just watched another heartbreaking TV photo-story illustrating the tragic reality of hunger in the Third World countries.

I wrench with guilt and compassion for those skeletonlike images that stare at me as I sit in front of the TV stuffing my mouth with abundant food. Lord, forgive me—but I can't intercede simply on the basis of guilt; nor do I see the entire Third World starvation problem simplistically reduced to the Scriptural image of a dehumanized Lazarus at the gate of Dives.[1] I have to pray in a different way after hearing a report from my friend, Walt. He approached the leadership of several Third World countries with a village-oriented food storage technology to prevent their often ample harvest from rotting, as has been the case over the last several years. He was turned down!

The problem is that villagers in several of these countries have a cultural tradition of storing their grains and foodstuffs under the floor boards of their houses until all decays. I pray for a breakthrough in the hearts and minds of those Third World people—that they may be willing to set aside some of their cultural practices and at least experiment with methods that would help keep them alive.

[1]Luke 16:20, *KJ*

NOW THERE ARE THREE

Lord, over the past few months I've been
thrilled by having close encounters with four
beautiful deer. I frequently see them at twilight,
grazing on a hillside. We glance at each other,
maintaining a respectable distance.

I praise You for them; they've learned to tolerate
me and to stand longer and closer each day
that I run past them. I "consider"[1] them marvel-
ous "works of Your hands"[2] that warm my heart
with their dignity, grace and beauty.

I've never felt any particular responsibility to
intercede for deer. They seem sufficient and
safe enough living off the land. That was until
yesterday! Suddenly there was an "out-of-
season" gunshot somewhere off in the distance.
And when it came time for me to rendezvous
with my animal friends later that evening, the
deer herd had been reduced to three.

From this point, Lord, I accept responsible
"dominion"[3] for the deer as I pray for their
protection against evil men who ruthlessly test
their rifle skills on unsuspecting animals out of
season.

Would it be all right to pray the 91st Psalm for
the deer?

[1]Luke 12:24 [2]Psalm 8:6, *NKJ* [3]Genesis 1:28, *NKJ*

NEEDED: SERVANTS

Lord Jesus, Your Word says You "humbled"[1] Yourself and took the form of a "servant."[2]

Shouldn't our relationship to the earth's delicately balanced ecosystem be that of a loving friend rather than a bulldozing maniac? Shouldn't having "dominion"[3] at this point in our planet's history be more priestlike as we bless the environment with tender, loving care?

O God, I pray for our earth home that's at such risk! Forests and vegetation are being destroyed by acid rain. Marine ecosystems are increasingly endangered by overfishing, pollution, and coastal builders. Whole species of plants and animals are becoming extinct because of human exploitation.

Lord, I hear You saying so plaintively, "They have made my pleasant portion a desolate wilderness."[4] Forgive us for the vacuous reasoning that *we* know more about the care of the earth than *You* do, when You have built into our creative life-forms such a finely-tuned support system of integrated control.[5] I intercede for our planet's created life: that we custodians at this late date become more custodial, like being available in helping You restore what we have ruined—which is the least we can do!

[1]Philippians 2:8 [2]Philippians 2:7 [3]Genesis 1:28, *KJ*
[4]Jeremiah 12:10, *KJ* [5]Genesis 1

PRAYER FOR RAIN

Lord, we need rain! I know that You are the author of everything that is "good";[1] therefore, the lack of rain is not to be laid on Your doorstep but that of Your enemy and my/our failure to intercede for our environment.

Therefore, in the name of Jesus, I bind the negative influence of Satan[2] that would restrict the rainfall we need. I hear You say through Jeremiah that it is You ". . . who gives rain."[3] I hear You say through Zechariah: "Ask the Lord for rain."[4] So I ask now, praying the words You gave David:

> You care for the land and water it; you enrich it abundantly. The streams of God are filled with water to provide the people with grain, for so you have ordained it. You drench its furrows and level its ridges; you soften it with showers and bless its crops.[5]

So I intercede—"boldly."[6] Lord, send Your jet stream to do what You've ordained—let the soft showers "bless" us! Praise You, Lord!

[1]Genesis 1:31 [2]Mark 3:27 [3]Jeremiah 5:24, *NKJ*
[4]Zechariah 10:1 [5]Psalm 65:9–10 [6]Hebrews 4:16, *KJ*

WHEN THE SUN SONG
WENT OUT OF STYLE

Lord, our dermatologist doctor-friend recently
was forced to close his practice to new patients.
He's in an overload situation—seeing too many
people with skin cancers. He warns us in every
way possible to: "Stay out of the sun!" "Use
sun-block!" "Don't stay out too long!"

But I love the sun—particularly the "glory"[1] of
it. Isn't the doctor really saying that there's
nothing wrong with the glory of the sun?—it's
just that the ozone layer that filters out danger-
ous ultraviolet light has become depleted,
rubbed thin by the chlorofluorocarbons from
our spray cans, air conditioners, styrofoam
products, plastics, etc.

Dear Lord, it's not that we don't know what
we're doing. We do! We've been warned repeatedly about the thinning of the ozone layer since
the early 1970's. When the Psalmist sang,
"Praise Him, sun and moon,"[2] did he ever think
his song would go out of style? I pray You will
plant in our minds ways to overcome our
common death urge.

[1] 1 Corinthians 15:41, *KJ* [2] Psalm 148:3

FARMING THE OCEANS

Lord, I pray that a growing multitude of people
will develop a sensitivity to the need for consci-
entious "stewardship"[1] over *all* the resources of
our planet.

I keep hearing people talk about colonizing
outer space; but I'm still hearing Your prior
command to have "dominion over . . . all the
earth."[2]

I pray for an increasing number of innovative
thinkers concentrating on how we can farm the
ocean bottoms—recognizing that two-thirds of
our globe is under water—to produce an incredible amount of available food to feed the world. I
also pray we may learn how to desalinate ocean
water economically so that starving people who
try to live on waterless deserts will be blessed
with lands that "blossom as the rose."[3]

[1]Luke 16:2, *KJ* [2]Genesis 1:28–29, *NKJ* [3]Isaiah 35:1, *KJ*

WHO'S RESPONSIBLE
FOR THE MESS WE'RE IN?

Father God, please forgive this presumptuous comment (though I'm sure You've heard it before), but there's a growing core of public opinion that holds You directly responsible for our current ecological crisis. They cite Your words in Genesis commissioning Adam and Eve:

> Be fruitful and multiply; fill the earth and *subdue* it; have *dominion* over the fish of the sea, over the birds of the air, and over every living thing that moves on the earth.[1]

They also recite Your words in the Book of Psalms:

> The heaven, even the heavens, are the Lord's; But the earth He has given to the children of men.[2]

But wait a minute; didn't You also say:

> The earth is the Lord's, and all it's fullness, The world and those who dwell therein.[3]

Now I am confused! Please straighten me out!

OK, You're saying I should put these two scriptures together—for they are parts of the same whole. The earth is Yours but You have leased

---

[1]Genesis 1:28, *NKJ* [2]Psalm 115:16, *NKJ* [3]Psalm 24:1, *NKJ*

it to us. We are caretakers of Your trust. Nothing has changed from the beginning. We've been given responsibility to care for the earth like it belongs to us, only to remember it doesn't!

Dear Lord, what a sorry bunch of caretakers we've been! Have mercy on us!

OFF ON A SPECIAL MISSION

Yesterday I sent my young friend off to the
Middle West as if he were going on a military
search-and-recovery mission. I hugged him and
promised he'd be in my prayers.

We talked about the critical importance of his
governmental assignment. He's searching for
water supplies, measuring what is available and
checking its condition.

Lord, I intercede for the entire human family
who've consistently poisoned nearly every
waterway in the world. Challenge us to treat
and conserve better what we already have; and
please, Lord, provide[1] us with a continuing
supply of safe water in the same way that You
provide for the "birds of the air," "the lilies of
the field," and "the grass of the field"[2] despite
our folly!

I pray for my hydrology-expert friend who is
both explorer and soldier—for searching and
examining water supplies, and by Your grace
fighting off the evil one who would withhold
from us Your reserves and exploit the enemy
who is often us.

[1]Genesis 22:14   [2]Matthew 6:26–30

TOWARD A PEACEFUL LIFE

Lord God, tonight I'm interceding for the President of our nation.

I'm instructed by Your Word to make "supplications, prayers, intercessions, and giving of thanks . . . for all who are in authority."[1]

I pray the President may be "hedged about"[2] by Your protecting presence;[3] that he be strengthened by "the blood of the Lamb"[4] and that he "walk in the light"[5] as he leads our nation that, thankfully, continues to support about 90 percent of the Christian missionary work in the world and prayerfully remains the strongest influence for human rights and freedom anywhere.

I pray that he will be open to the full "counsel"[6] of Your will so that our nation and all nations have the opportunity of living "a quiet and peaceable life in all godliness and reverence."[7]

[1]1 Timothy 2:1–2, *NKJ* [2]Job 1:10 [3]Isaiah 43:2
[4]Revelation 12:11 [5]Ephesians 5:8, *KJ* [6]Proverbs 11:14, *KJ*
[7]1 Timothy 2:2, *NKJ*

FOR THE CHILDREN

Lord God, today I'm standing in the gap—
interceding for the dying children on our planet.
I'm positioning myself on Your word that with
You "nothing is impossible."[1] A while back I saw
the impossible happen when nations all over
the world, including both the United States and
the Soviet Union, joined creative forces, direct-
ing an avalanche of resources in attempting to
free two whales from an arctic ice field.

Each day the world watched the incredible take
place as international co-operation flourished,
helping two sea mammals escape to the open
sea.

Far more importantly, I'm praying for 40,000
children who are doomed to die today and every
day. O God, I pray that an international effort
be rallied to save each day's 40,000 children
dying, mostly in Third World countries.

By human calculation it seems impossible that
a unified effort of this magnitude could be put
together . . . that would transcend ingrained
political selfishness. Nevertheless, I'm standing
on Your word for the world's dying children that
"nothing is impossible" for You.

Help me pray for us!

[1]Luke 1:37

TREES AND MORE TREES

Lord, I just saw a man planting trees. Praise God! I intercede for our planet—with the "vision"[1] of a great throng of people out planting 720,000 square miles of new forests all over the world that'll remove a billion tons of carbon dioxide from the atmosphere each year.

It's only a "mustard seed,"[2] beginning to reverse the reckless destruction of trees that You put here to help maintain our delicate balance of life.

I pray You bless this vision as I stand interceding in "the gap"[3] as a "steward"[4] . . . with a trust and some seedlings and a shovel.

[1]Joel 2:28 [2]Mark 4:31 [3]Ezekiel 22:30, *KJ* [4]Titus 1:7, *KJ*

This book was produced by the Christian Literature Crusade. We hope it has been helpful to you in living the Christian life. CLC is a literature mission with ministry in over 45 countries worldwide. If you would like to know more about us, or are interested in opportunities to serve with a faith mission, we invite you to write to:

Christian Literature Crusade
P.O.Box 1449
Fort Washington, PA 19034